KNOW IT ALL
CASTLES

By Louise Nelson

BookLife PUBLISHING

©2022
BookLife Publishing Ltd.
King's Lynn, Norfolk
PE30 4LS, UK

All rights reserved.
Printed in Poland.

A catalogue record for this book is available from the British Library.

ISBN: 978-1-80155-615-6

Written by:
Louise Nelson

Edited by:
William Anthony

Designed by:
Dan Scase

All facts, statistics, web addresses and URLs in this book were verified as valid and accurate at time of writing. No responsibility for any changes to external websites or references can be accepted by either the author or publisher.

PHOTO CREDITS

All images are courtesy of Shutterstock.com. With thanks to Getty Images, Thinkstock Photo and iStockphoto.
Front cover: 3drenderings, Archiwiz, josefauer, Kletr, Sergiy1975, Brian Kenney, Gary Perkin, 3DMI, Marti Bug Catcher. 4&5 – Marti Bug Catcher, Guryanov Andrey, Gwoeii, PRESSLAB, Mr Doomits, Fer Gregory, Kletr, canadastock, Matt Gibson, Greig Gallagher, Harveychl. 6&7 – LifetimeStock, faestock, Nejron Photo. 8&9 – LifetimeStock, Marti Bug Catcher, ChameleonsEye. 10&11 – vvoe, PRESSLAB, Patryk Kosmider, Billy Stock, VectorMine, JeniFoto, Helen Hotson, Guillaume Rey, 3DMI, Phil Friar, kerryhilden. 12&13 – Dronegraphica, IR Stone, Tomas Marek. 14&15 – faestock, Nejron Photo, Jopics, Momentmal, haeton, IR Stone. 16&17 – sidmay, Gallinago_media, Edward Westmacott, Nik Merkulov, Volodymyr Horbovyy, Olga Popova, Nejron Photo. 18&19 – Kondor83, MaraZe, 3DMI, Kai Beercrafter. 20&21 – BasPhoto. 22&23 – m.o.arvas, Kovtun Dmitriy, James Steidl, Cherednichenko Aleksandr. 24&25 – Esteban De Armas, ch123, LiskaM. 26&27 – Cedric Weber, JuliaST, Wondering Green Man, lehic, lrpizarro. 28&29 – pzAxe, xpixel, Patricia Snircova, Alinute Silzeviciute. 30&31 – Pond Thananat, VOJTa Herout, Roop_Dey, RobertHur, Adrian Stanica. 32&33 – Andre Goncalves, Sport08, Sytilin Pavel, Laurence D. Matson, Mikhail Novokreshchenov, Marti Bug Catcher. 34&35 – Sofia Kozlova, Karramba Production, Cernecka Natalja, strogaya, Anton Starikov, Vac1, faestock. 36&37 – Sunndayz.

CONTENTS

Page 4	**Castles**
Page 6	**Key Ideas**
Page 8	**What Are Castles?**
Page 10	**Timeline: Castles**
Page 12	**Types of Castle**
Page 14	**Life in a Castle**
Page 16	**Food and Drink**
Page 18	**Health and Hygiene**
Page 20	**Case Study: Windsor Castle**
Page 22	**Attacking a Castle**
Page 24	**Siege!**
Page 26	**Defending a Castle**
Page 28	**No More Castles**
Page 30	**Castles around the World**
Page 32	**Believe It or Not!**
Page 34	**Activities**
Page 36	**Quick Quizzes**
Page 38	**Glossary**
Page 40	**Index**

**Words that look like this can be found in the glossary on page 38.
Key ideas you will need can be found on page 6.**

CASTLES

Princesses, dragons and medieval knights... These might spring to mind when we think of castles. We see castles in movies and on TV all the time. But even if the fairytales are fantasy, the buildings themselves are real!

So, what do you think of when you think of a castle?

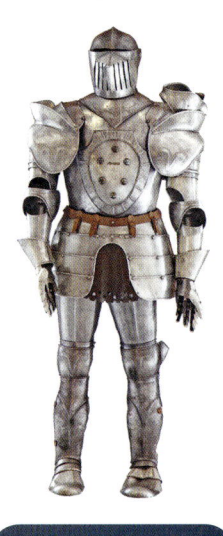
KNIGHTS

ARCHERS

TREASURE

WEAPONS

ROYALTY

TURRETS AND TOWERS

DEFENCES

DIAOYU CASTLE, CHINA

BODIAM CASTLE, ENGLAND

NEUSCHWANSTEIN CASTLE, GERMANY

Castles are found all over the world, from China to the UK, and each one had many uses. For hundreds of years, castles were homes, meeting places, defences and ways to show how rich and powerful the owners were. They were places of business and places of war.

EDINBURGH CASTLE, SCOTLAND

KEY IDEAS

Here are some key words and ideas you need to know when reading this book. Read them through before you start, then check back here if you need to remember.

ROYALTY AND MONARCHY

Every country has a **system** for who is in charge. A monarchy is one of these systems. In a monarchy, a family is the ruling family, and the head of that family is the king or queen. They are also in charge of the country. Everyone in the ruling family is considered royalty, including princes and princesses. When the ruler dies, their children will be the next kings or queens.

NOBILITY

Other powerful and important families were known as the nobility. People of nobility were considered better than other people and were born into important families. Dukes, duchesses, countesses and barons are all **ranks** of nobility.

THE MIDDLE AGES

The Middle Ages in Europe was a period of time between the years of 476 and 1485. It is also known as the medieval period. This time is famous for the Black Death, a terrible plague that swept through Europe.

WHAT ARE CASTLES?

Castles are buildings that were built for important people such as royalty or nobility to live in, and they were **fortified**. This means they were built with defences to protect the people inside if they were attacked.

Kings and queens often built grand castles to show how important they were.

Castles often had strong walls and were difficult to attack.

Castles were popular in the Middle Ages. Over a period of about 900 years, lots of castles were built, mostly in Europe and the Middle East. Castles could be built of wood or stone. As new **technology** was developed over time, the way castles were made changed.

Castles were often built in areas that were difficult to reach.

JABREEN CASTLE, OMAN

'Burg' is German for 'castle'.

BURG ELTZ, GERMANY

A fortress is a building for defence, but no one lives there. A palace is a home for important people, but it does not have defences.

TIMELINE: CASTLES

THE IRON AGE

Hill forts made of wood were a village's best defence...

...until their enemies invented fire-arrows.

AROUND 1000

Smaller buildings, such as houses, were kept safe behind a wall, in an area called the bailey.

SIEGE!

SIEGE TOWER

Many weapons were built to try to damage and attack castles, too.

AROUND 1270

Concentric castles have a keep, an inner wall and an outer wall. Attackers would have to get through both walls to reach the bailey and the people inside.

AROUND 1400

HERSTMONCEUX CASTLE, ENGLAND

The fort is now known as a keep and can be made of wood or rough stone.

NORMAN KEEP AT CARDIFF CASTLE, WALES

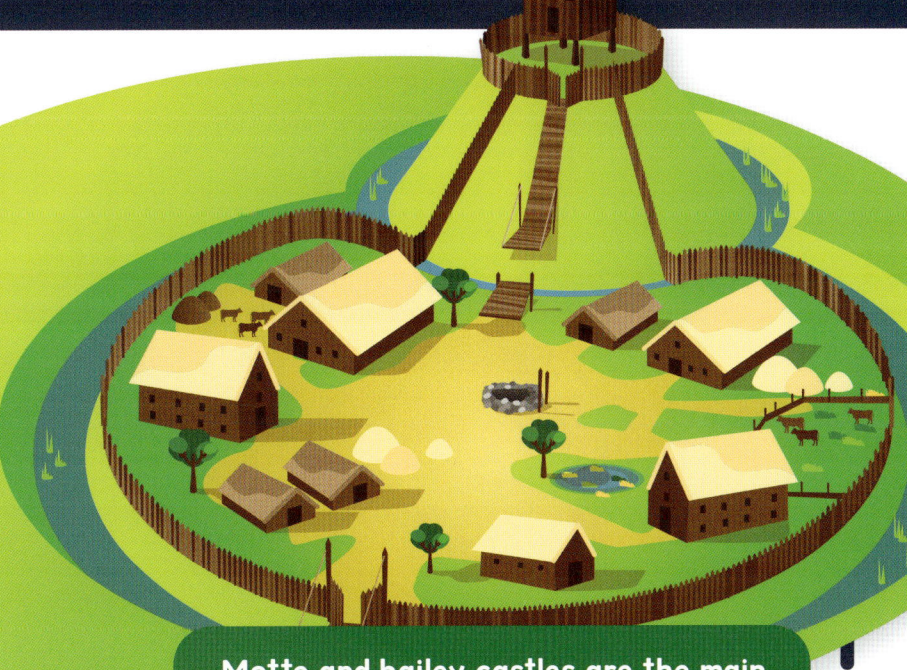

Motte and bailey castles are the main type of castle being built at this time.

AROUND 1070

Round keeps were easier to defend.

William the Conqueror built square, stone keeps with turrets and towers. The walls were extremely thick.

THE WHITE TOWER, TOWER OF LONDON, ENGLAND

AROUND 1550

Castles became status symbols instead of fortresses. The nobles made their castles bigger, more comfortable and more like fancy homes... with a few defences, just in case. These are called fortified manor houses.

WALMER CASTLE, ENGLAND

No one needed castles inland anymore – the nobles had stopped fighting each other. But they were still fighting France, and several castles were built to defend the south coast.

TYPES OF CASTLE

MOTTE AND BAILEY CASTLES

These castles had two parts. The wooden keep was built on a raised mound of earth called a motte. This meant that you could see attackers coming. It is also easier to defend if you are higher than your enemy. The steep banks were known as a scarp.

The houses, stables, kitchens and workshops were in a lower yard surrounded by a wall, called a palisade. This is the bailey.

STONE KEEP CASTLES

Later motte and bailey castles had stone keeps. While motte and bailey castles made of wood could be built quickly and were not meant to last, stone keeps were built to stand for a lifetime. Stone keeps were strong and could be tall and impressive. Stone keeps were not **vulnerable** to fire.

ROCHESTER CASTLE, ENGLAND

CASTLE ACRE, ENGLAND

KEEP

SCARP

MOTTE

BAILEY

PALISADE

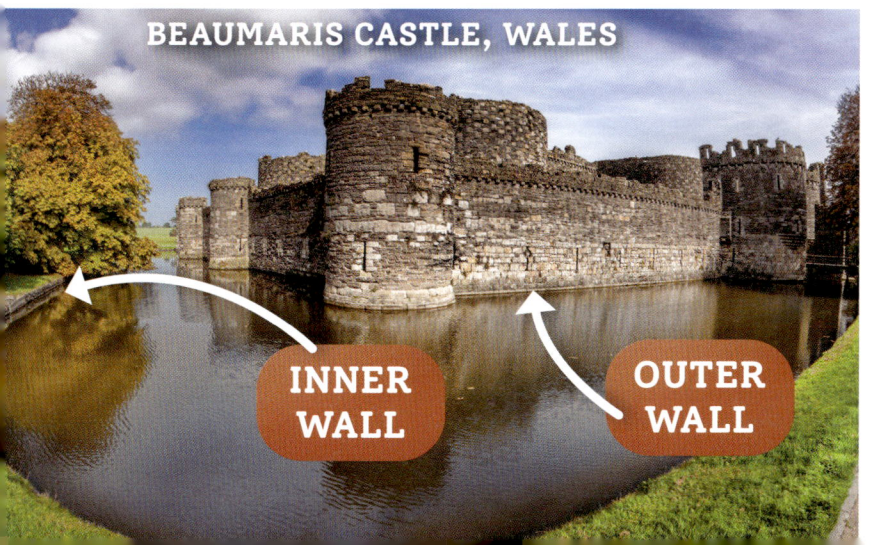

BEAUMARIS CASTLE, WALES

INNER WALL

OUTER WALL

CONCENTRIC CASTLES

Concentric castles were stone castles with at least two walls surrounding the bailey. You can think of this like a castle inside a castle. The outer wall was usually shorter than the inner wall. These castles were very difficult to attack.

LIFE IN A CASTLE

Castles may have been fortresses, but they were homes too. Many people lived and worked in a castle. During peacetime, castles would have been the centre of the local area, busy with people going about their lives. During war or siege, people would have moved into the castle for protection.

Royalty and nobles would have had <u>luxury</u> apartments in the keep.

Soldiers lived together in the castle, in an area called a barracks. Their job was to defend the castle and act as a sort of police force.

Some servants had bedrooms to share, but many would sleep wherever they could. The worst job went to the lowliest servant, called the gong farmer. Their job was to empty out the toilets!

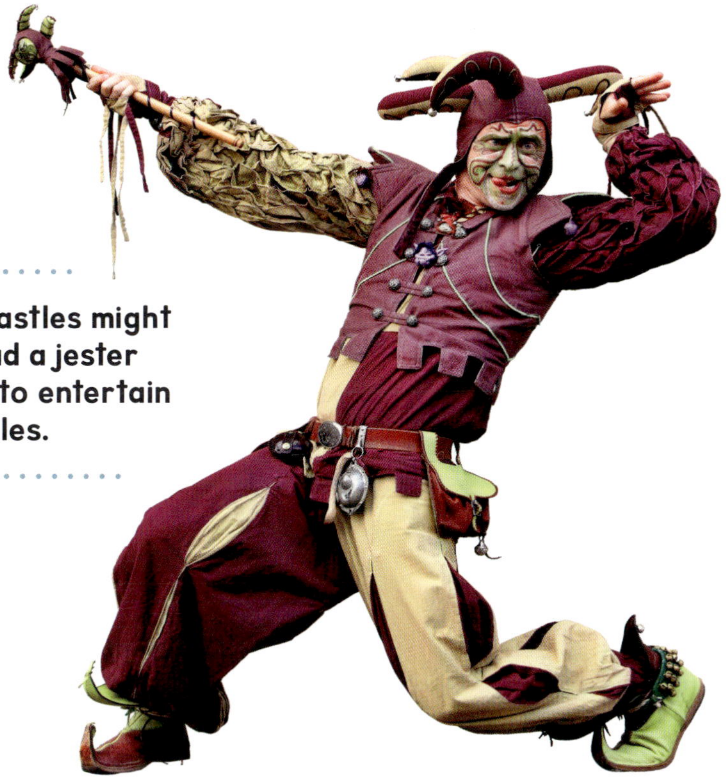

Many castles might have had a jester or fool to entertain the nobles.

The children of other nobles were often sent to work at a castle, serving the king and queen. This was to help them learn courtly manners and meet important people.

Castles would have been busy, bustling places full of people working and living their lives.

FOOD AND DRINK

The busiest person in a castle was probably the cook. The cook might have had to feed hundreds of people in a day or create a grand feast for important guests at a moment's notice!

But what would they have eaten?

In the Middle Ages, people ate many things that we do not today – including swans!

There were no fridges, so fish and meat was <u>preserved</u> for the winter using salt.

Spices were very expensive in the Middle Ages. Using these showed off how wealthy the owners of the castle were.

Water was often too foul to drink. Ale and wine were popular choices instead.

A flat piece of <u>stale</u> bread, called a trencher, was used as a plate, then given to peasants or horses to eat. Later, metal and pottery plates were used.

For a special occasion, a banquet might be prepared. The best meats, cheeses and fruits from the land owned by the nobles would be cooked and beautifully presented.

DID YOU KNOW?

The kitchen was a busy place. Kitchens were locked at night to stop servants stealing food and wine!

HEALTH AND HYGIENE

In medieval times, doctors did not have the same medicines we have today, and there were no hospitals. People didn't understand germs. They thought that illness came from bad smells.

Toilets in a castle were usually just a hole, opening into a pit or directly into the water below.

Richer people often had bad teeth, because they could afford to eat sugar. People would rub their teeth with a cloth or a hazel twig to clean them.

Fleas were a big problem. They lived in straw bedding and on animals.

Plague was a serious illness that killed lots of people. Plague doctors wore masks with long beaks that were filled with spices and oranges. This made it so that bad smells could not get to them, which they thought would stop them from getting sick.

MEDIEVAL medical instruments

DID YOU KNOW?

When the gong farmer collected the poo from the toilets, they would often spread it on the fields to **fertilise** the crops!

Surgery in medieval times was pretty brutal. There were no painkillers, so a wounded person would be advised to get very drunk before an operation!

Baths were taken only a few times per year. It was a lot of work to collect and heat that much water – remember, there were no taps! Most people washed their hands and face each day in a bowl.

CASE STUDY: WINDSOR CASTLE

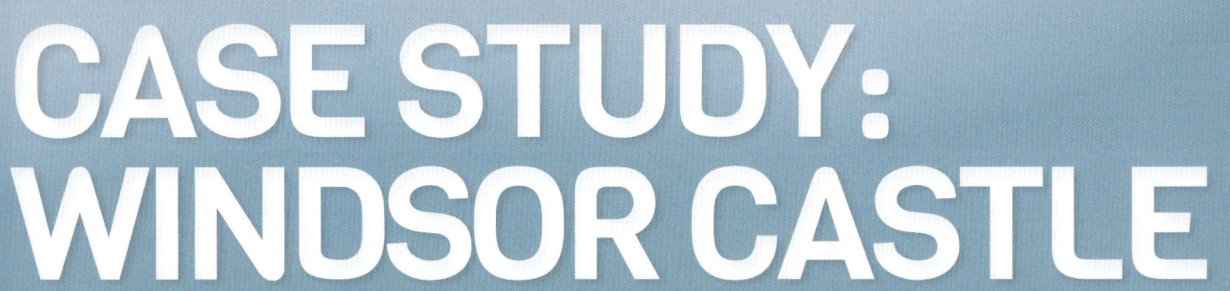

Windsor Castle is in England. It was built by William the Conqueror, and the head of the British royal family lives there today. It is the largest castle in the world to still have a monarch living in it.

Windsor Castle is a motte and bailey castle. It was built on the banks of the River Thames. Over the years, the castle has been repaired and rebuilt. The castle was rebuilt in stone by Henry II.

Many monarchs have lived here, including Henry VIII, Elizabeth I, Queen Victoria and Elizabeth II.

ATTACKING A CASTLE

Castles were fortresses for a reason. Because a monarch or important person lived there, and all the treasure was there, enemies had many reasons to want to attack. In the early days of wooden motte and bailey castles, the easiest way to attack a castle was with fire. Flaming arrows could fly over your palisades and set the keep alight without a single enemy soldier needing to get over the walls.

Stone castles don't burn very easily. So, to take over a castle, you've got to get through the walls. Early stone walls could eventually be torn down with pickaxes. As walls got thicker, armies would dig underneath the walls and blow them up! This is called undermining.

Catapults and other heavy weapons were used to throw large stones at the walls. If you could make even one hole, you could get your soldiers inside to fight.

A battering ram like this one could swing its enormous weight into the doors and gates of a castle. These were often weak points, but were heavily guarded.

DID YOU KNOW?

Soldiers could put ladders against the walls and try to climb over, too. The goal was to get your soldiers inside somehow, while the enemy did their best to keep you out!

23

SIEGE!

A very effective way to capture a castle was a siege. In a siege, an army would surround a castle, and no one would be allowed in or out. Then, the attacking army would simply wait. It might take weeks, or even months, but the goal was that eventually the people would starve and be forced to surrender.

During a siege, as your enemy became weaker, you would carry on trying to get inside. Siege weapons were built. These were huge weapons that were designed to either break down the walls or get your soldiers inside.

Inside a castle under siege, people were forced to eat horses and even rats.

A trebuchet used a long arm and a swinging motion to throw rocks at high speeds.

A siege tower could be pushed up against the walls. Soldiers could climb up inside, safe from enemy arrows, and get into the castle.

DID YOU KNOW?

In a siege, catapults and trebuchets were used to throw other things, too. Dead animals, the bodies of plague victims, poo and even the heads of captured soldiers were all thrown into the castle. This was done to scare and upset the people inside, or make them all very sick!

25

DEFENDING A CASTLE

Castles are built for defence. Most are built in places that are hard to reach. Some are by rivers, the sea or special ditches filled with water, called moats. The walls are high and thick. The windows are very small, just wide enough for an archer to shoot through. These are sometimes called arrow slits or loops. Castles are often built on hills, and have tall turrets and towers so you can see any enemies coming.

PORTCULLIS

ARROW SLITS

MACHICOLATIONS

If any enemies did get close enough to attack, gates would be closed and a portcullis would be drawn. This was a special metal gate that covered the wooden one. Boiling oil, flaming arrows, poo, boiling water and other horrible things could all be thrown at enemies from above, through special holes in the walls, called machicolations.

DID YOU KNOW?

Machicolations are also known as murder holes.

Crenelations were these tooth-shaped gaps. Archers could hide while shooting at the enemy scaling the wall, or pour boiling water onto soldiers scaling ladders.

NO MORE CASTLES

Eventually, **gunpowder** was invented and cannons became the new weapon of war. Cannons could launch huge cannonballs at enormous speeds. Even strong castle walls could not stand up to that for long. Long sieges were a thing of the past. War, and the world, had changed.

Cannons were built bigger and bigger over time.

Cannonballs were made of metal. They were very heavy and hard. These were much more effective than big rocks.

The castles left standing were either abandoned or changed into fancy homes. Monarchs then only used castles as status symbols, to show off how much money they had.

Many castles were left to fall apart. These are called ruins.

Castle Drogo was built between 1910 and 1930. It was the last castle to be built in England.

Today, many castles still stand, hundreds of years after they were built. Lots of them are cared for by **historians**. If you are nearby, you can visit them to get a sense of life inside their giant stone walls.

Himeji Castle in Japan was built for samurai warriors. It is a maze of buildings, walls and gates, and the keep in the centre is six **storeys** tall!

CASTLES AROUND THE WORLD

Neuschwanstein Castle in Germany is said to have inspired famous stories and films.

Mehrangarh Fort still stands proudly above the city of Jodhpur, India. It was built from red sandstone.

Chapultepec Castle is in Mexico. Today, it has a history museum inside.

DID YOU KNOW?

Author Bram Stoker used pictures and descriptions of Bran Castle in Transylvania to imagine the castle of his most famous creation… Count Dracula!

BELIEVE IT OR NOT!

Let's take a look at some amazing facts about castles.

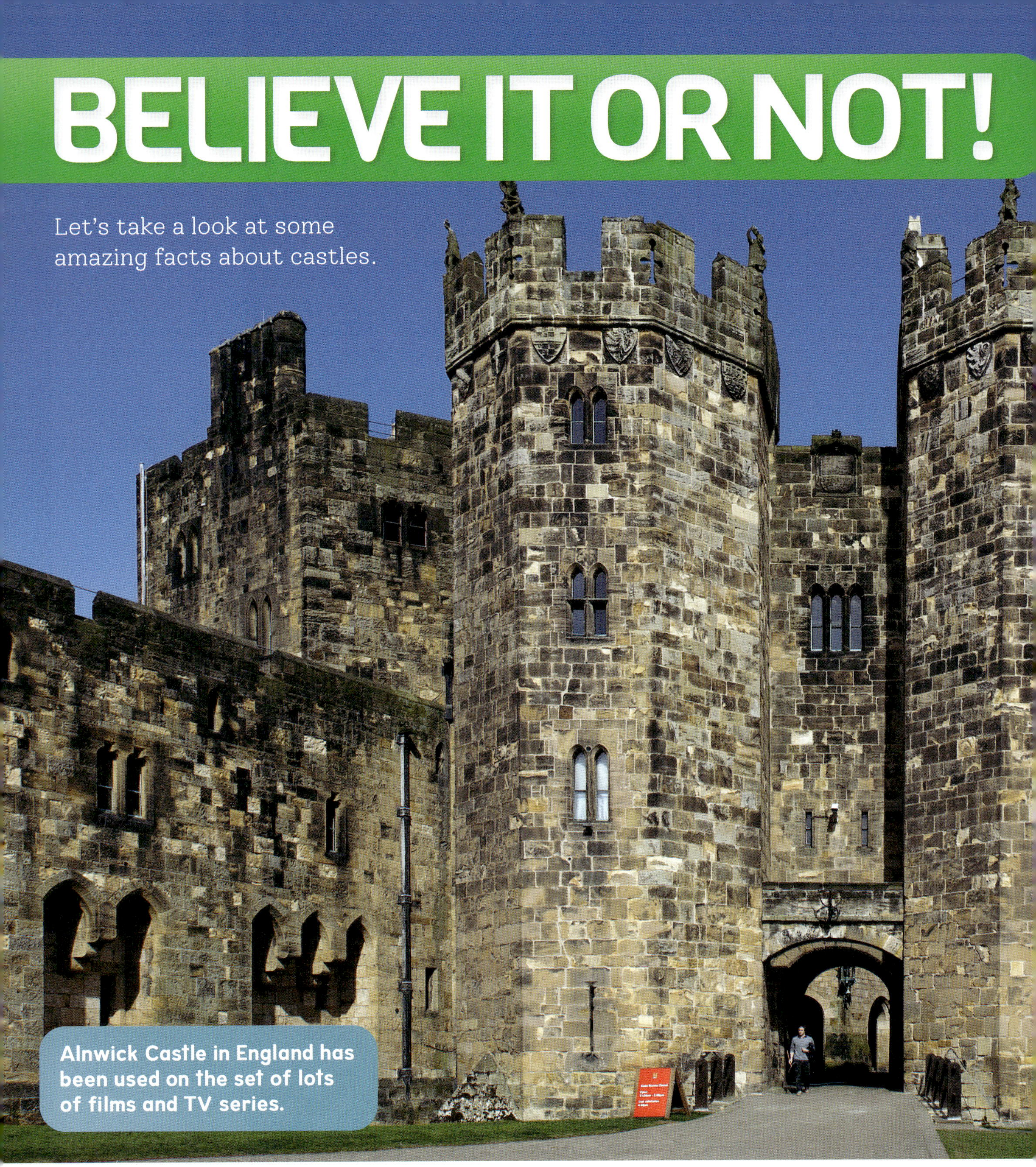

Alnwick Castle in England has been used on the set of lots of films and TV series.

Stairs in castles are tight spirals moving upwards in a clockwise direction. Invading soldiers would have to fight upwards, which is harder. They wouldn't be able to swing their swords in such a tight, curved space, and they would have to use their swords in their left hands.

GARDEROBE

Many toilets in castles were simple holes built into the walls. You sat over a little hole in a special area called a garderobe, and your poo and wee would fall through the hole directly into the moat! Yuck!

There are thousands of castles in England still standing.

Dover Castle, on the south coast of England, wasn't just a medieval fortress. It was used as a base in both World War One and World War Two.

33

ACTIVITIES

Can you complete these fun activities?

BE A CASTLE ARCHITECT

Grab some paper and pens, and imagine you are a noble or monarch. You're going to build a new castle to live in. Remember, your castle needs to keep you safe, but also show your friends how powerful and fancy you are. What will you include on your castle? Remember, you're the most powerful person around, so you can have whatever you want!

Will your castle be a modern marvel or a medieval masterpiece?

MYTHS AND LEGENDS

Many castles have inspired fairytales, myths and legends. Can you write a story with a castle at the centre? Will you write a scary story, like Bram Stoker's *Dracula*, or a fairytale? Will your castle have wizards and dragons, or a spooky ghost roaming the corridors? Is your story set in the past, when the castle was in its full glory, or set now, in the crumbling ruins? Get creative!

Look at the features of these castles. Can you spot two that are the same?

Answer: 12 & 14

QUICK QUIZZES

Can you beat our terrific tests? 3... 2... 1... GO!

MEMORY TEST

Can you answer these questions? Check back through the book if you're not sure.

1. What is this weapon called?

2. What is the German word for castle?

3. What is a motte?

4. Which type of castle had at least two sets of outer walls?

5. Whose job was it to empty poo from the toilet pits?

POP!

Pop quiz question! Which castle is the largest castle still occupied today? Who lives there? Check page 20 for the answer!

Answers: 1. Catapult 2. Burg 3. The raised mound where the keep is built 4. Concentric castles 5. The lowliest servant, known as the gong farmer.

36

POINT IT OUT

Point to these parts of the castle.

BANNERS

CRENELATIONS

KEEP

OUTER WALL

MOAT

ARROW SLITS

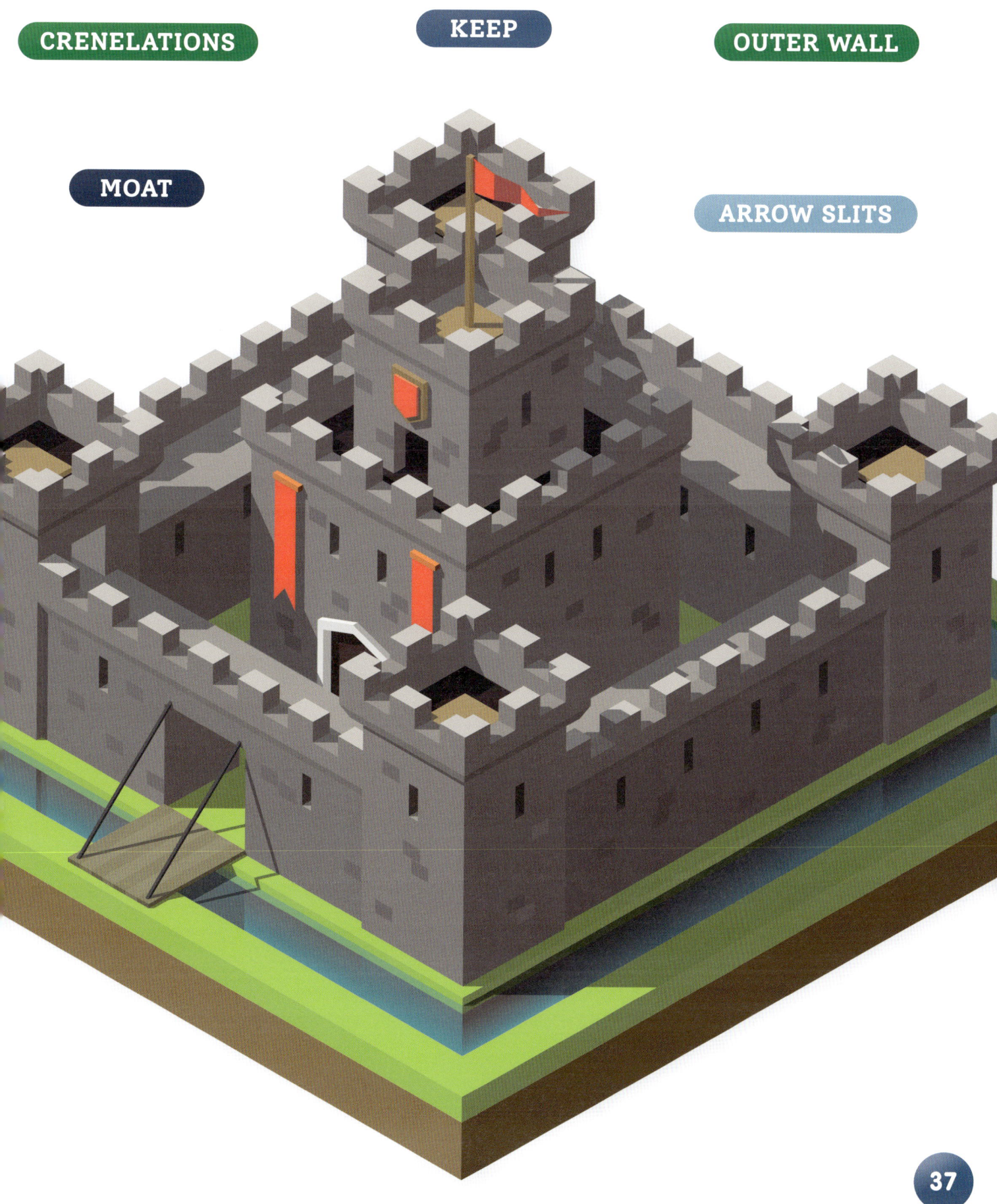

GLOSSARY

C
concentric to have the same centre

D
defences things used for protection

F
fertilise to make a plant or flower able to produce seeds

fortified made stronger, usually by using a defence

G
gunpowder something that explodes when it is touched by fire

H
historians people who look at what happened in the past to find out about it

L
luxury something that is expensive and of a high quality

M
medical instruments tools that are used by doctors, nurses and surgeons

N
Norman relating to the people from northern Europe and France who conquered England in 1066

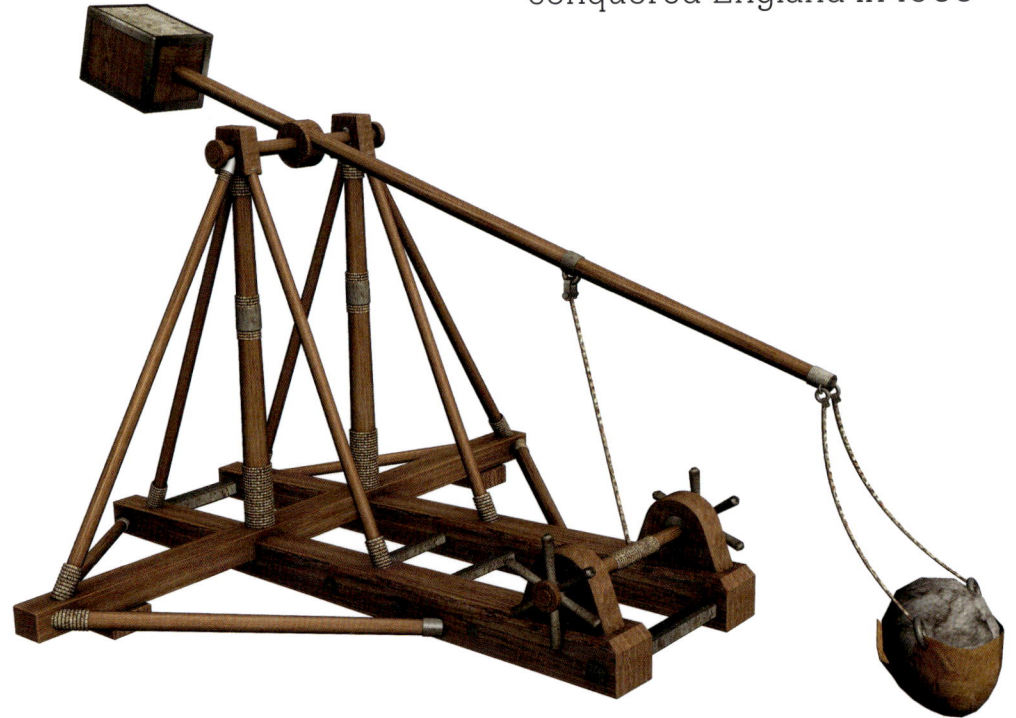

P

preserved kept in good condition over a long period of time

R

ranks levels within a community that are based on how important someone is

S

stale no longer fresh

storeys single floor levels of a building

system a group of related parts, people or ideas that work together

T

technology things that are useful and can be used to solve problems or make things

V

vulnerable easily hurt or harmed

INDEX

A

armies 23–24

B

baileys 10–13, 20, 22

banquets 17

barracks 14

baths 19

battering rams 23

boiling oil 27

C

cannonballs 28

cannons 28

catapults 23, 25

concentric castles 10, 13

cooks 16

D

defences 4–5, 8–12, 14, 26

F

fleas 18

fortresses 9, 11, 14, 22, 31, 33

G

gong farmers 14, 19

H

hill forts 10

J

jesters 15

K

keeps 10–14, 22, 30, 37

M

machicolations 27

manor houses 11

moats 26, 33, 37

mottes 11–13, 20, 22, 36

murder holes 27

N

nobility 6, 8, 11, 14–15, 17, 34

P

palaces 9

palisades 12–13, 22

peasants 17

plagues 7, 19, 25

portcullises 27

R

royalty 4, 6, 8, 14, 20

S

scarps 12–13

servants 14, 17

siege towers 10, 25

siege weapons 24

soldiers 14, 22–25, 27, 32

spices 16, 19

stone keep castles 11–12

sugar 18

T

teeth 18

trebuchets 25

W

walls 8, 10–13, 22–30, 33, 36–37

war 5, 14, 28, 33